KATIE LEDECKY

by James Buckley Jr.

Consultant: Ellen Labrecque
Former Editor and Writer
Sports Illustrated for Kids

BEARPORT
PUBLISHING

New York, New York

Credits

Cover, © Qi Heng/Xinhua/Alamy Live News; 4, © Marcos Brindicci/Reuters/Newscom; 5, © Stephen Wermuth/Reuters/Newscom; 7, © Mo Khursheed Media via AP; 8, © Andrew Weber/USA Today Sports; 9, © Mike Lewis/ZUMA Press/Newscom; 10, © Jorge Silva/Reuters/Alamy Stock Photo; 11, © ZUMA Press/Alamy Stock Photo; 12, © Michael Sohn/AP Photo; 13, © Michael Sohn/AP Photo; 14, © Giuliano Bevilacqua/ABACAPRESS.COM/Newscom; 15, © Qi Heng/Xinhua/Alamy Stock Photo; 16, © Chine Nouvelle/SIPA/Newscom; 17, © Stanislav Krasilnikov/Itar-TASS Photo Agency/Alamy Live News/Alamy Stock Photo; 18, © Rob Schumacher/USA Today Sports; 19, © USA Today Sports; 20L, © jejim/Shutterstock; 20R, © Zach Bollinger/Icon Sportswire via AP Images; 21, © Jacklyn Lippelmann; 22TL, © Jorge Silva/Reuters/Alamy Stock Photo; 22TR, © Tombaky/Dreamstime; 22B, © FisherPhotoStudio/Shutterstock; 23, © Chine Nouvelle/SIPA/Newscom.

Publisher: Kenn Goin
Senior Editor: Joyce Tavolacci
Creative Director: Spencer Brinker
Production and Photo Research: Shoreline Publishing Group LLC

Library of Congress Cataloging-in-Publication Data

Names: Buckley, James, Jr., 1963– author.
Title: Katie Ledecky / by James Buckley Jr.
Description: New York, New York : Bearport Publishing, 2018. | Series:
    Bearport's Library of Amazing Americans | Includes bibliographical
    references and index. | Audience: Age 5–8.
Identifiers: LCCN 2017010892 (print) | LCCN 2017012281 (ebook) |
    ISBN 9781684022946 (Ebook) | ISBN 9781684022403 (library : alk. paper)
Subjects: LCSH: Ledecky, Katie, 1997–Juvenile literature. | Women
    swimmers—United States—Biography—Juvenile literature. |
    Swimmers—United States—Biography—Juvenile literature. | Women Olympic
    athletes—United States—Biography—Juvenile literature. | Olympic
    athletes—United States—Biography—Juvenile literature.
Classification: LCC GV838.L43 (ebook) | LCC GV838.L43 B84 2018 (print) |
    DDC 797.2/1092 [B] —dc23
LC record available at https://lccn.loc.gov/2017010892

For more information, write to Bearport Publishing Company, Inc., 45 West 21st Street, Suite 3B, New York, New York 10010. Printed in the United States of America.

10 9 8 7 6 5 4 3 2 1

CONTENTS

Unstoppable

It was the 2016 Olympics. Katie Ledecky shot through the water. She was swimming the 800-meter **freestyle** race—her best **event**. Everyone was amazed by her speed. Some of the other swimmers were an entire **lap** behind her! Would she win gold?

Katie launches into the water at the start of the race.

Katie was far ahead of the other swimmers during the 800-meter freestyle.

The 2016 Summer Olympics took place in Rio de Janeiro, Brazil.

Into the Pool!

Katie Ledecky was born on March 17, 1997, in Washington, DC. She grew up in Bethesda, Maryland. Her mom and brother were both swimmers. Before long, Katie became a swimmer, too.

Katie loved being in the pool. Sometimes, she swam 40 miles (64 km) in a single week! Katie was so fast that by high school, she was breaking U.S. records.

Katie also enjoys playing the piano and Irish dancing.

Katie celebrates winning the 2011 Junior National Championships!

A Big Splash

In 2012, Katie **competed** for a spot in the Olympics. She was only 15 years old. To everyone's surprise, she won the 800-meter freestyle. That meant Katie was headed to the Olympic Games in London!

Katie at the 2012 Olympic Trials, which were held in Omaha, Nebraska

Katie surged through the water to make the Olympic team.

In swimming races:
200 meters = 4 laps
400 meters = 8 laps
800 meters = 16 laps
1500 meters = 30 laps

Golden Moment

Katie was the youngest American Olympian in London. During the 800-meter race, she won a gold medal! Plus, she set a new U.S. record. "I knew if I put my mind to it, I could do it," Katie said.

Katie shows off her Olympic gold medal.

President Barack Obama

After the Olympics, Katie and the U.S. team met President Barack Obama.

Record Breaker

While Katie was still in high school, she kept swimming—and winning! At the 2013 World Championships in Spain, she set a new world record in the 800-meter freestyle. She also won three gold medals there.

In 2013, Katie won the World Swimmer of the Year award.

Katie is overjoyed after breaking a world record at the 2013 World Championships.

World Champ

Two years later, Katie set three more world records! She was the second person ever to hold the 400-, 800-, and 1500-meter world records at the same time. She also won five more gold medals. Katie was unstoppable!

Katie dives into the pool.

Katie has the 10 fastest times ever recorded in the 800-meter freestyle.

Katie turns her head to the side to take a breath.

Off to Rio!

Before the 2016 Olympics, Katie was nervous. She would be competing against the best **athletes** in the world. Katie started the Games by winning a silver medal in a **relay**. Then she won gold in the 200- and 400-meter swims! That left the 800-meter race.

Katie celebrating the relay win with her teammates

The Olympics includes 34 swimming events.

Katie (right) and her teammate Leah Smith (left)

17

Best Ever

In the 800-meter final, Katie won by 11 seconds! She beat her own world record, too.

Katie finished the Rio Olympics with four golds and one silver. That was the best ever for an American woman. "I'm just so happy," Katie said.

Katie cried tears of joy at the medal ceremony.

Katie's world-record time in the 800 meter was just 8 minutes and 4.79 seconds.

The Future

After the Olympics, Katie finished high school. Then she attended Stanford University and joined their swim team. Naturally, she kept winning and setting records.

Katie has her eye on more gold medals at the 2020 Olympics in Tokyo, Japan!

Katie wore one of her Olympic gold medals at a swimming event at Stanford.

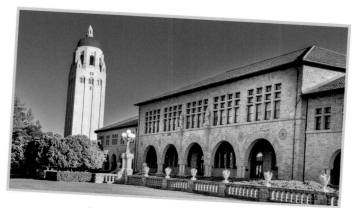

Stanford University

In 2016, Katie visited her grade school in Maryland. She hoped to inspire future athletes.

Timeline

Here are some key dates in Katie Ledecky's life.

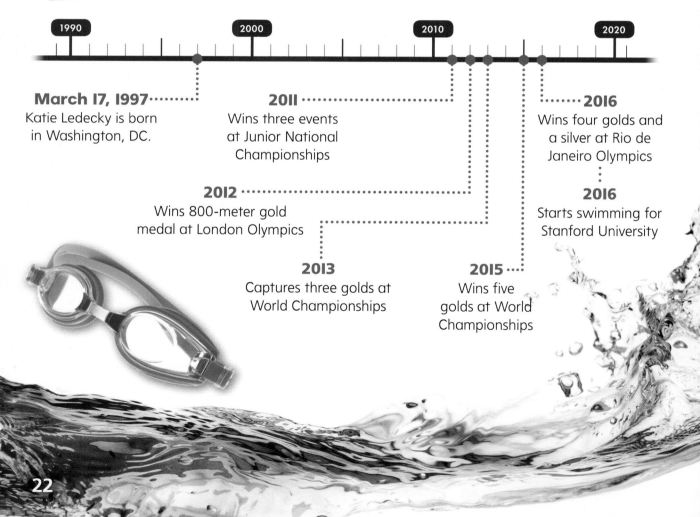

1990   2000   2010   2020

March 17, 1997
Katie Ledecky is born
in Washington, DC.

2011
Wins three events
at Junior National
Championships

2012
Wins 800-meter gold
medal at London Olympics

2013
Captures three golds at
World Championships

2015
Wins five
golds at World
Championships

2016
Wins four golds and
a silver at Rio de
Janeiro Olympics

2016
Starts swimming for
Stanford University

Glossary

athletes (ATH-leetz) people who are trained in sports

competed (kom-PEET-ed) took part in a contest

event (ee-VENT) a single race at a swimming meet

freestyle (FREE-stile) an event in which swimmers can choose any stroke; a stroke that includes alternating overarm movements and a flutter kick

lap (LAP) the distance from one end of a pool to the other

relay (REE-lay) a swimming race in which four teammates take turns swimming laps

Index

Read More

Lajiness, Katie. *Katie Ledecky (Big Buddy Olympic Biographies).* Minneapolis, MN: Big Buddy Books (2016).

Scheff, Matt. *Katie Ledecky (Olympic Stars).* Minneapolis, MN: ABDO (2016).

Learn More Online

To learn more about Katie Ledecky, visit
www.bearportpublishing.com/AmazingAmericans

About the Author

James Buckley Jr. has written dozens of books about sports for young readers.